Ion Pandele

Mother America

Poems

PublishAmerica
Baltimore

© 2006 by Ion Pandele.
All rights reserved. No part of this book may be reproduced, stored in a retrieval system or transmitted in any form or by any means without the prior written permission of the publishers, except by a reviewer who may quote brief passages in a review to be printed in a newspaper, magazine or journal.

First printing

At the specific preference of the author, PublishAmerica allowed this work to remain exactly as the author intended, verbatim, without editorial input.

ISBN: 1-4241-1991-X
PUBLISHED BY PUBLISHAMERICA, LLLP
www.publishamerica.com
Baltimore

Printed in the United States of America

To my wife

Tattoo

Look at my tattoo
It's like a taboo,
All this useless skin
Can go in that bin.
We are all the same,
Different by name,
But I have no brother,
Just my mom and father,
The rest are all strangers,
Like for wolf the rangers.
Now I have this look,
A new way of hook,
You can read in me,
Is all I want to be,
No matter I'm small
The tattoo takes all.

01.13.05, Tampa

The Rain

It's raining steadily and slow,
The grass has drowned into the ground,
I wish to sleep, I don't know,
Or just to look from that blue mound.

The birds are sailing in the sky
Between dark drops and lightnings,
The sunset is on standing by
To cover all with black large rings.

It's wet deep down and mud and sick,
Above is a giant transparent bell,
The roads are just a mess and slick,
Should be much better in the hell.

I feel I'm swimming in my eyes,
Somewhere people work like shadows
To stick in water plants of rice,
The mist is covering the meadows.

It seems like perpetual this rain,
I just can't handle any more, you see
Is melted even the Death's chain,
Dead bodies are floating next to me.

                              01.14.05, Tampa

Hula Hoo

Hip hop
Horoscope,
Click set
Internet,
Rick'a boom
No room,
Kiss criss
Vis-à-vis,
Hula hoo
Déjà vu,
Shake dade
Mascarade,
Itchy ushion
Prostitution,
Via mia
Bulimia,
Flick flock
Roll and rock,
Hory rory
End of story.

                                  01.14.05, Tampa

So Good So Far

So good so far
Look at my scar,
So far so good
I'm like in a hood

So good so far
What's a good car?
So far so good
Look at my mood.

So good so far
Too late for a star,
So far so good
Don't be rude.

So good so far
Let's go to a bar,
So far so good
See you later, dude.

                          01.24.05, Tampa

Money, Business, Fame

It's a crazy world around,
We think we are all the same,
Is something else to be found,
A blessing we think, but shame,
Money, business, fame.

What's true and where's the lie?
Just a few are in that Guiness
And all sooner or later we'll die,
Still there is a kind of fairness,
Money, fame, business.

Some people lost everything,
For a few is just milk and honey,
Yet the fortune means nothing,
Don't think the wolf is a bunny,
Business, fame, money.

So we go back to the beginning,
A good life some will acclaim,
There is another hidden feeling
That we are guilty and insane,
Money, business, fame.

                          01.24.05, Tampa

Revenge

In my life I was unfair humiliated,
My dear friends were the enemies,
The patience is now terminated,
It is time to pay back all these.

I tried to help other people in need
And to share my love and my heart,
But tired, finally I had to concede,
All my trust was just falling apart.

Despite all the adversity I try again,
Is never too late to defend and win,
Doesn't matter is something to gain,
Trust in God and whisper: Amin!

Now is the moment for my revenge,
I will curse the world with my poetry
And with sweet stanzas I will avenge
All the years lost in a hostile society.

I will bury with flowers all my foes,
To make real peace I will endeavor,
The snobbery will be under my shoes,
The Art is my punishment forever.

                                        01.26.05, Tampa

Who I Am

I am not a poet, not even an American,
But just a painter and I am Romanian,
I escaped from communism barely alive
And the golden dream didn't really arrive,
A good life for me here wasn't mean to be,
Worse than all, my people cheated on me.
I tried to bring beauty in a material world,
Money is important, the rest is just a word,
I was in the ghetto with thieves and whores
Waiting for someone to open some doors,
A lot of hard working as I'm doing now,
Still I am looking for that success: how?
Finally I realized my effort was in vain
And I got nothing but frustration and pain,
Then, the time passed years over my head,
So I can see the end of the tunnel ahead.
But you know something? I trust in Lord,
For sure He has for everybody a sword
To judge and punish and make a justice,
The ultimate day will come without notice.
For me it's simple, I have nothing to lose,
The art was the way I accepted to choose,
I will die poor, alone and unheard, I know,
But maybe in the sky there is for me a row,
I will fly between bright stars in the Universe
Where the money or the fame have no sense.
Everything is just spirit, silence and serenity
My soul will be free, a shadow of humanity.

                      01.28.05, Tampa

A Gap

There is a gap in the ground
No fountain is to be found,
There is a gap deep in the sea,
The sharks have no right to plea,
There is a gap in the big cloud,
The sound of thunder is so loud,
There is a gap straight in the sky,
A reason for the birds to be shy,
There is a gap in my shoulder,
Isn't good to be hit by a boulder,
There is a gap through my eyes,
I can't see playing the dice,
There is a gap right in my heart,
Why am I stupid and not smart?
There is a gap right into my soul,
I am trapped in an invisible bowl.

      01.30.05, Tampa

Lonely

We are lonely in this world of ours,
Lonely we live, lonely we die slow,
Time is measuring years and hours,
Closer we come to the end of the show.

There is so much fun and people around,
Life is full of friends and pleasures,
But everything will be buried in the ground
Before even starting to take any measures.

While we are young is so hard to think
The road of life is too short, that's sad,
Between school, work we barely blink
To see the truth which are driving us mad.

So what's life, is this good or wrong?
Why we have to die and not live long?
These questions are like drums in a song,
God has the answer and keep us strong.

Maybe we'll receive help from some pals,
No way, they love the money, we are alone
Just like a leaf in autumn which quietly falls
Upon a soul resting for ever under a stone.

       01.30.05, Tampa

Just a Dream

For every poor people all around
There is a dream for good and hope,
America is the most beautiful sound,
Everyone is like freed from a rope.

This large country is a real dream
The supreme goal is to reach its land,
But for the most there is cry and scream,
They have no chance until the end.

For me, as I can see I should be proud,
I'm living all that dream right here,
I love America but I have to speak loud
Because is still injustice, poverty and fear.

From outside we see skylines and style,
But from inside the ghetto and no hope,
It's like we are stirred in a gigantic pile,
Just a few can survive to reach the top.

Let's put in this way, it's a kind of contest,
From all the challengers just one will win,
The rest are losers, what they can request?
The same like for America: is just a dream.

                                      01.31.05, Tampa

Teach Me

I'll ask the birds: teach me to fly,
I want to be an arrow in the sky.

I'll ask the fish: teach me to swim,
The same like a shark, fast and slim.

I'll ask the cheetah: teach me to run,
In savanna, just follow the path of sun.

I'll ask the nightingale: teach me to sing,
For the ears and soul, what a sweet sting.

I'll ask the camel: teach me to survive,
Despite the obstacles, a winner I'll arrive.

I'll ask the wolf: teach me how to scare,
Enemies who stay against me, try to dare.

I'll ask the owl: teach me to be smart,
To show how is to have a true heart.

I'll ask the buffalo: teach me to be strong,
To smash around what's bad and wrong.

I'll ask the lion: teach me to be a king,
The whole world will obey at my ring.

01.31.05, Tampa

Ding Dong

Ding dong
Sing a song.

Cling ling
Bell the ring.

Bing bang
Cut the gang.

Rim ping
Be a king.

Clic clock
Rock'n rock.

Stick stash
In a flash.

Dic dock
Off the frock.

Bim bam
Kick Saddam.

Tip top
Is no hope.

Bee gee
Not for me.

                         02.03.05, Tampa

So Old and Poor

I am so old and poor,
The life is too short, for sure,
I'd like to return before
But I can't be young any more.
Only the memory may stay,
For the rest we have to pray.
Who's the enemy, the friend?
Maybe we'll know in the end,
Something is outside, yes,
But better look inside, I guess,
It depends on us to be good
To behave in the neighborhood.
I was trying to survive,
Here I am folks, still alive,
For how long, I don't know,
God keeps the record of the show,
I can say just straight and bold
That I am so poor and old.

                                      02.20.05, Tampa

We Are Immigrants

We are immigrants, yes I know
To America we have little to show,
Except to look hard for a lousy job
And exposed to the merciless mob.

We come from all over the globe,
With another culture and language,
In this new society we have to probe
That we can carry the same luggage.

We are immigrants, yes and we love
It's just about normal human feelings,
At the same time we pray and starve,
May God bless our few belongings.

How is for us working on this land?
Just patience and sweat and desire,
For every right we have to stay stand
To fulfill the justice we like to aspire.

Not all the Americans like us, it's true,
They forget they were immigrants once,
Together in the history we can go through
And the future will be good for all of us.

We are immigrants, yes and we want
To be citizens in America, that's for sure,
Our love for this country is a warrant
And we can help, even we are so poor.

We don't speak English, it's not a shame,
Everything can be learned, we are friends,
United we put America in the hall of fame
To keep the freedom forever over the ends.

02.27.05, Tampa

Be Happy in America

The world belongs to the stars,
The celebrities make all the rules,
We just work and heal our scars
And then applaud like the mules.

You don't have money or got sick?
Doesn't matter, even there's no food,
Just turn on the TV and press, click,
In Hollywood some people feel good.

The screen is like a mirror of magic,
Is fascinating to watch so funny stuff,
The life is happy, no trace of tragic,
But somewhere the things are tough.

So, what about the rest of us, all,
The majority, losers, we get nothing,
We don't need to read the crystal ball
To see our future is not like of a king.

We should be happy, and why not?
Here is a pretty life, job and car,
The American dream is only a spot
In the ocean, but for us is good so far.

Too many people work too hard,
This is the problem, that's not fair,
A few blessed live in a golden yard
While the rest just struggle in despair.

Is good to be in America, of course,
But is better to enjoy the freedom too,
To have a status, not a deterred course,
Not even rich, happiness can touch you.

02.27.05,Tampa

Dead End

A jaw
Is not a paw
The tooth
Is not smooth
A claw
Is not a bow
The spear
Has no fear
The gun
Is not for fun
A dead end
Is not a friend
A tomb
Is not a room
A grave
Isn't so brave
A knife
Is not a life

                                04.15.05, Tampa

I like Tomatoes

I confess, I have a weakness
Since I was a kid, I like tomatoes,
In my country the life was expensive
Only the communism was extensive,
But I had a pleasure, just to eat
Tomatoes, and they were cheap.
I came in America with big goals
But the road was full of potholes,
The only thing I wanted so bad,
To don't feel lonely and sad
Was to eat tomatoes, fresh and nice,
Like the Chinese eating the rice.
I love America, is a wonderful land,
Even I feel like I am second hand,
Everything is cheap, houses and cars,
You can afford to go even on Mars,
To buy tomatoes, this is a dream,
I'm going crazy and ready to scream,
I want to eat tomatoes like in the past,
But I can't and the price is up so fast…

04.16.05, Tampa

Update

Global warming is on the rise,
An African took finally the Nobel prize,
Most of Romania was destroyed by hail,
Martha behaved like a heroine in jail,
Children are starving to death in Sudan,
Billions are lost in Iraq and Afghanistan,
The doctors say that HIV is under control,
Wall Mart is opening mall after mall.
The chicken flu is not spreading again,
While the desert is flooded by the rain.
Summer is here, we adjusted the hour,
The donuts are not sweet, but sour.
In China were buried alive a lot of miners,
Who said the homeless are not losers?
The Russians killed an American journalist,
Viagra is the most wanted item on the list.
No crap, we'll have forever a young face,
The plastic surgery is going to win the race,
The industry will build a new update car
An atomic one, no gas to pay so far.

04.30.05, Tampa

No More

I can see red flames in the dark,
There are gaps in the recent history
Sealed with a chain of blooded mark,
It's time now to reveal that mystery.

We think that we live in prosperity,
The past is over and the injustice away,
The most important is to have the liberty,
But we can't just forget and pray.

Some people are suffering right now
Because the parents, siblings were killed,
And they ask the question: why and how?
It's possible the justice to be fulfilled?

I can see flames, after all these years,
No more burning crosses, no more racism,
In America and Europe, no more tears,
No more nazism, no more communism!

Let's learn this very painful lesson well
And open for peace a brand new door,
Another mistake can send us to hell,
To war, hatred, crime we say: no more!

                        06.12.05, Tampa

Candor

Young ladies walk in the park with candor,
You can admire them, what a splendor,
Life is so beautiful, just honey and milk,
Their hair is shining in the sky like the silk.

Then the divas crossed together the street,
It's time for a snack, so "bonne apetite."
Rustling nostrils and hungry blue eyes
Are devouring hot dogs and french fries.

At the same time a truck is passing near by,
Packed with calves which traveled to die,
A few hours after, the animals will be killed
In the slaughter house where fates are sealed.

Now the girls put new lipstick on their lips
And start to walk again, waiving their hips,
From the calves the blood is flowing in rivers,
The meat is ready to go for the hamburgers.

The odyssey of the hungry ladies is over,
They are so candid, like a beautiful cover,
But, some innocent animals, on the other side
Are taking with no candor, the ultimate ride.

06.18.05, Tampa

Why

Why the water is wet?
Why there are holes in the net?
Why the desert is dry?
I'm asking myself, why?

Why the earth is round?
Why the water is not the ground?
Why we can't touch the sky?
I'm asking myself, why?

Why the earthquake is shaking?
Why the liar is faking?
Why "hi" is not instead "bye?"
I'm asking myself, why?

Why the Universe is unlimited?
Why the people is not united?
Why the deep is not high?
I'm asking myself, why?

Why the money is power?
Why the salt is so sour?
Why to sleep is not to die,
I'm asking myself, why?

06.18.05, Tampa

My Dog

My dog is my master,
His name is Casper,
I'm happy and proud
When is barking so loud.
I'm thinking in the end
He's my ultimate friend.
Take Casper far from me,
You just can't, you'll see.
I share with him everything,
Even without a pot Ming,
I'm taking good care of him,
For me is like a sun beam.
In this crazy world and mad,
I feel just upset and sad,
The most important thing,
It's having my dog and sing.
This is all about and the above,
My dog, unconditional love.

06.26.05, Tampa

The Big Bird

We like to see small ducks,
We like to see chickens,
Some people like to hunt bucks,
But be aware if you take aboard
And trust the big bird.

I saw with my own eyes
That big bird eating baby ducks
And chickens, like french fries,
These babies of the water world
Are a prey for the big bird.

This is the balance of nature,
Maybe, even I don't like it at all,
It's sad to kill a helpless creature,
I wish to have a long sharp sword
To show to that big bird.

I can do nothing but to write
And to express my sincere sorrow,
I wish this victims to try to fight,
Unborn ducklings I have a word,
It's coming the big bird.

                        06.27.05, Tampa

Find Yourself

We are lost like in a jungle,
It's hard to find the right way,
Try to listen and be humble,
If there is trouble, go away.

This is our society, whatever,
Some are fortunate, mostly not,
The rule of law will last forever,
A common people is just a knot.

You have to try to fight hard,
Find the enemies and the danger,
Protect yourself like your yard,
And sharpen a long dagger.

Before starting this big crusade,
It's better to look all around,
Find yourself, a drop in a cascade
And listen to your destiny's sound.

7.10.05, Tampa

Taking the Pills

I'll teach you how to take the pills
Don't go over the top of the hills,
If you feel sick from that disease
Just smile and say a word: cheese.
Go to the doc and ask him straight,
But for the cure you have to wait,
He will prescribe some medication
And you can go to your destination.
The best is to don't need all these
But live in a good health and peace,
The doctor can heal you temporary
Even will finish all in the mortuary.
Sometimes the life is like a limerick,
Or better "to be or not to be" sick,
It's simple, you have to understand,
Even taking pills you come to an end.

                                        07.10.05, Tampa

One, Two,...

One, two, three,
Jump over the tree,
Two, three, four,
Keep opened the door,
Three, four, five,
Drive is not to dive,
Four, five, six,
Break it first, then fix,
Five, six, seven,
It's long way to Heaven.
Six, seven, eight,
I can see no weight.
Seven, eight, nine,
Everything is mine,
Eight, nine, ten,
Just give me a pen.

                    07.11.05, Tampa

Dig Deep

Dig deep into the ground,
Stop the pendulum sound.
Dig deep into the ocean,
Stop the perpetual motion.
Dig deep into the sky,
Stop the hurricane's eye.
Dig deep into your brain,
Stop if you know a name.
Dig deep into you heart,
Stop at the love for the Art.
Dig deep in your soul,
Stop if you reached a goal.
Dig deep into your past,
Stop to wipe out the dust.
Dig deep into your future,
Stop at the destiny's picture.

                        07.14.05, Tampa

The Sweet Smell of Corn

I love shopping at the produce market,
There is everything to put in the basket,
From all the vegetables I prefer corn,
It's like I see the place where I was born.

I grab the fresh corn and I smell it,
For my remember is a perfect fit,
I figure out the cornfield so green,
Like a rain forest on a giant screen.

Valleys and hills covered with corn,
The nature has it's way to adorn
Our land, and I tell you something,
In the country side, the corn is a king.

Now I'm in America, I can't complain,
I still love to see the corn in the rain,
When was the time for me to be born,
Was coming over a sweet smell of corn.

> 07.16.05, Tampa

Feel Free

I wish to write expressive poetry
To show the spirit's immortality,
I wish to find wonderful words
To connect two different worlds,
I wish to unveil metaphoric verses
To build a bridge over the courses,
I wish to do all these, but I can't
Because I am just an immigrant,
But you have to know something,
America for me is everything,
Since I was a kid far away I knew
I will come all the way through,
The problem is about my language,
It's not like to change a luggage,
Even so, I love so much this land
That I'll do my best until I'll stand,
It's important for me I feel free here
So I can speak my way without fear,
I wish the same for the folks around
To share in peace a common ground,
What can I say in the end to thee,
That's all I want my friend, feel free.

     07. 16.05, Tampa

Signs

Death is not such a bad thing
No trespassing
There is no miracle medication
No solicitation
Everybody thinks is a king
No loitering
Even in anger, don't shout
No way out
It's really tough to be a champ
No ramp
Put the glasses, then start to read
No speed
Young people are good looking
No smoking
For life there is a legacy
No vacancy
Every mountain has a hiker
No biker
Pong is the last name of ping
No dumping
Don't expect something in return
No turn

                    07.23.05. Tampa

Flea Market

There's a place to eat junk food
Right in the flea market hood,
Tasty crispy sweet angel wings
And large roasted onion rings.
Kings and queens, their fate
You can end with a check mate.
Toys, balls and gloves for boys,
Dolls, flowers is the girls' choice,
Fragrance, furniture, new or old,
Paper, fabric, tin, silver and gold,
CD's, DVD's, incents and food,
Good taste, bad taste or just rude,
Paintings, kitsch, Chinese stuff,
Even something pretty rough,
I feel good, is like in my country,
Kind of you are going to a party.
There is everything in the world
From cockatoos to a ninja sword.
Let me tell you something cool,
There is an alligator in the pool,
Big stores are for the rich for sure,
Flea market for guys like me, poor.

                        07.24.05, Tampa

Some Presidents

Just some good health
For president Roosevelt,
The war is not human
For president Truman.
Balance is a power
For president Eisenhower,
A crisis is not a remedy
For president Kennedy.
Sing a Vietnamese song
For president Johnson,
Don't try to cheat on
For president Nixon.
Have a good word
For president Ford.
Is fair even a charter
For president Carter,
Earth is not a heaven
For president Reagan.
Try to don't push
For president Bush,
Life is still going on
For president Clinton.

08.16.05, Tampa

I'm Tired

I'm tired to drive a junk car
I'm tired to work hard so far
I'm tired about the communism
I'm tired to live in capitalism
I'm tired to listen the propaganda
I'm tired with the VIP's agenda
I'm tired of sickness and poverty
I'm tired to find a cheap property
I'm tired to fulfill my dreams
I'm tired to believe by all means
I'm tired to fear of the terrorists
I'm tired of all kind of specialists
I'm tired to see famine in Africa
I'm tired being tired in America
I'm tired to be alone and bold
I'm tired to put my future on hold
I'm tired to pray for my health
I'm tired to wait for the death
I'm tired to be an ethnic American
I'm tired being born a Romanian.

08.16.05, Tampa

The Same Routine

We go to the job and pay the bills
Like bikers climbing the same hills,
It's really hard to keep up and strain
A cold feeling in the shade of a chain.
Work and work then driving so fast
The future is going back in the past,
Then little relaxation and the TV set,
A dinner, a paper, maybe the Internet,
This is our life, full of sick passion
But in fact is a complete concession,
We give up our ideals and main goal
It remained so little to enjoy the soul,
There is even no time to really think
Our balance is on the edge of a brink,
Everything is about job and money
Doesn't matter it's raining or sunny,
What's the Nature, a piece in a puzzle
Already tired we feel like a dazzle,
Anyway it's not important, the best
Is to take a short break and just rest,
The next day should be like any other
Just look forward and don't bother,
I look like a robot, a human machine
Doing my duties, the same routine.

                              08.26.05, Tampa

Internet

It's cool browsing the screen
I love the Internet
And plenty of junk to be seen
I hate the Internet
Tired after my job I feel fresh
I love the Internet
But for that I pay with cash
I hate the Internet
It is like a wonderful world
I love the Internet
A hacker has a hidden sword
I hate the Internet
Babes and games are for free
I love the Internet
In the end they ask you a fee
I hate the Internet
I can see myself right there
I love the Internet
My business is going nowhere
I hate the Internet
Come on, is just like a window
I love the Internet
Just see but don't try to follow
I hate the Internet

09.04.05, Tampa

Up and Down

Look at me, I'm good and strong
I'm down, baby, I'm up
But I can't keep it all day long
I'm up, baby, I'm down
You are more precious than gold
I'm down, baby, I'm up
No change for me, poor and old
I'm up, baby, I'm down
God gave me talent, I love the art
I'm down, baby, I'm up
The lack of money is the sad part
I'm up, baby, I'm down
I offered you my love and blessing
I'm down, baby, I'm up
In time my power will be ending
I'm up, baby, I'm down
Baby, you are everything I have
I', down, baby, I'm up
There is nothing I can save
I'm up, baby, I'm down
With you I will die like a brave
I'm down, baby, I'm up
Just put some flowers on my grave
I'm up, baby, I'm down…

09.07.05, Tampa

My Friend

My friend has no face
My friend has no race
My friend is not famous
My friend is not jealous
My friend has no feeling
My friend is not stealing
My friend is not funny
My friend is not dummy
My friend has no heart
My friend doesn't do art
My friend is not a monster
My friend is not blockbuster
My friend doesn't play
My friend doesn't obey
My friend doesn't cook
My friend is just a book
My friend is a visionary
My friend is a dictionary

09.08.05, Tampa

I Can See

I can see blood
I can see tears
It's so much flood
So many fears

I can see hate
I can see injustice
Kind of a cursed fate
Full of malpractice

I can see poverty
I can see pain
Should be a serenity
Drowning in the rain

I can see war
I can see extremism
Life is a whore
In totalitarism

I can see corpses
I can see fever
There are dead horses
Floating on the river

09.10.05, Tampa

What We Have

We have one life,
Let's live with honor.
The life is not so long,
Don't waste the time along.

We have one goal,
Let's be happy and succeed.
Be prepared for the worst,
Try to fight against you first.

We have one talent,
Let's share with the others.
Money, business are useless,
The art and beauty are priceless.

We have one God,
Let's trust and pray.
Just think will come the end,
After that, it's nothing to spend.

We have one death,
Let's die in dignity.
She can take our body away,
But not our spirit, no way.

                                           09.11.05, Tampa

Mother America

I came from far a long way
To spend my life here and stay,
Even I didn't have too much fun,
Mother America, I'm your son.

I dream to climb your mountains,
To search all the surroundings,
On the beaches I'd like to run,
Mother America, I'm your son.

I 'm talking to brothers around
And enjoy the birds' divine sound,
The misery and sorrow are gone,
Mother America, I'm your son.

I work hard but I don't complain,
I want my life to be with no stain,
I will fight, even I have no gun,
Mother America, I'm your son.

I wish to be better, to live longer,
Teach me to be smarter, stronger,
Between all you are like the sun,
Mother America, I'm your son.

      09.11.05, Tampa

Miracle

Poetry for the spirit is everything
And is coming from nothing.
I'd like to try here to confess,
This is a miracle, I guess.

Don't just look at the words,
It's kind of the song of the birds,
You wish your soul to express,
This is a miracle, I guess.

Every night is dark in the sky
Suddenly colored flames may fly,
It is aurora borealis, priceless,
This is a miracle, I guess.

Remember Moses with his choice
The stone was chiseled by a voice,
God wanted through him to address,
This is a miracle, I guess.

The talent and poetry are divine,
Like the sun they forever will shine,
Let's be immortal one moment, yes,
This is a miracle, I guess.

       09.12.05, Tampa

My Vision

Honesty, integrity, respect,
These are my values.
Work, talent, passion,
This is my vision.
Patience, belief, resilience,
This is my philosophy.
Optimism, serenity, kindness,
This is my view.
Truth, fairness, charity,
This is my opinion.
Love, friendship, compassion,
These are my feelings.
Art, poetry, modesty,
This is my talent.
Money, hypocrisy, loneliness,
This is my curse.
Beauty, balance, wisdom,
This is my goal.
Cooperation, challenge, tolerance,
This is my conclusion.

                                          09.13.05, Tampa

Life Is a Race

Life is a race
Keep up the pace
You have to run
To have some fun
When you stay
You have to pay
If you are slow
You have to grow
If you are fast
Forget the past
If you are right
Have a good sight
You may love or hate
This is your fate
You may win or lose
Don't hold it loose
You may live or die,
Sorry, there's no tie.

                          09.17.05, Tampa

Rembrandt

Who's Rembrandt? Of course, we know
But I want something else to show,
He wasn't only a painter but a rich guy
And his wife was like a star in the sky.
Well, the life was in this case complete:
Fame, money, even the style was obsolete.
Just like that all these changed one day,
Saskia and the kids just passed away,
The only ship he owned sunk in the sea,
What was left: just sorrow, misery to see.
Remember the kings in the early ages,
We barely read their names on old pages,
But Rembrandt is different, we can enjoy
His art and our life is fulfilled with joy.
After wealthy years, he was sick and poor,
He proved the spirit is important, for sure,
We inherit a fortune, this is the only truth,
His soul and vision are coming through.
Let's learn from this old masters dean,
The great Rembrandt Harmensz van Rijn.

                             09.17.05 Tampa

The Summer Is Over

The summer is over,
The sun is gone,
It's coming October—
Sorry, no more fun.

The summer is over,
It's time to chill,
Let's be just sober
And take a pill.

The summer is over,
There is steady rain,
Looks like moreover
We'll go insane.

The summer is over,
That's it, so what!
Look for some cover,
Protect your butt.

The winter is coming,
Now is a new order—
Sneezing and freezing,
The summer is over.

                    09.19.05, Tampa

Remember New Orleans

Destructive winds, disaster, flood,
Demolished houses, homeless, blood,
Chaos, abandoned kings and queens,
Remember New Orleans!

A whole tragedy, pain and despair,
Floating bodies, hunger, choking air,
Thousands of evacuees, lost teens,
Remember New Orleans!

A history collapsed, memories shattered,
The city is a ghost, its soul is scattered,
Instead of cars, mangled parts and rims,
Remember New Orleans!

Behind all these we face human nature,
Corruption, hypocrisy, the dark feature
Of politics, God is punishing our sins,
Remember New Orleans!

Above this colossal nightmare is a hope,
There were people saved just with a rope,
A lot of help and courage, by all means,
Remember New Orleans!

09.20.05, Tampa

My Hands

I love my hands since I was a boy,
They were so small, just like a toy,
And later much stronger, my friends,
Yes, look at my hands.

It came a time when with a sad hand
I buried my dear father at his end.
The fingers were crying, my friends,
Please, look at my hands.

Then I was holding my future wife,
So happy hands, so beautiful life,
God is great, let's pray, my friends,
Amen, look at my hands.

And next, the most beautiful thing
To push my baby girl in a swing,
My palms were proud, my friends,
Try to look at my hands.

Now I have bruises and scratches
And spots like burned matches,
This is my old skin, my friends,
Just look at my hands.

       09.24.05, Tampa

Masks

We use to wear a mask
When we approach a task,
We want to be in control,
No drop of sweat to fall.

Having good sight, behind
Maybe we are just blind,
A nice face, with twinkles
Can hide deep wrinkles.

Sometimes we show joy,
Instead is a mask for decoy,
We smile with admiration
While there is frustration.

Playing all the time and fake
We are lost, for God's sake,
These masks finally will go,
No real face for us to show.

      09.24.05, Tampa

The Cutting of the Diamond

Deep inside the dark ground
There's no gold to be found,
Just fire, hell and high pressure
Not even a trace of a treasure.

And yet it is something there,
A small crystal we like to share,
After millenniums in the mud,
A flame is growing like a bud.

First we need to dig quite long
And keep the will pretty strong,
If we are very lucky, in the end
We can be happy, my friend.

We hold in our hands a stone,
There's no need to dig or roam,
It's time for the multifaceted cut,
Then the diamond will look hot.

Our life is like this crystal, uncut,
All we need is to do the right cut,
The spirit will be pure and clever,
A perfect diamond, clear forever.

09.24.05, Tampa

An American Citizen

I came here a long time ago,
It was so much fear to undergo,
Now I can freely speak loud
I'm humble, I'm honored, I'm proud.

The life was first pretty tough,
I didn't expect my way to be rough,
I was patient and I don't mumble,
I'm honored, I'm proud, I'm humble.

All I want is to be a good citizen
And I expect nothing in return,
I wish with honesty to be covered,
I'm proud, I'm humble, I'm honored.

I'm so happy, living like a dream,
A new American praying an hymn,
My soul is clear, not even a cloud,
I'm humble, I'm honored, I'm proud.

      09.24.05, Tampa

List of poems

Tattoo
The rain
Hula hoo
So good so far
Money, business, fame
Revenge
Who I am
A gap
Lonely
Just a dream
Teach me
Ding dong
So old and poor
We are immigrants
Be happy in America
Dead end
I like tomatoes
Update
No more
Candor
Why?
My dog
The big bird
Find yourself
Taking the pills
One, two
Dig deep
The sweet smell of corn
Feel free
Signs
Flea market
Some presidents
I'm tired

The same routine
Internet
Up and down
My friend
I can see
What we have
Mother America
Miracle
My vision
Life is a race
Rembrandt
The summer is over
Remember New Orleans
My hands
Masks
The cutting of the diamond
An American citizen